BELVEDERE

a brief history

by

JOHN A. PRICHARD

LONDON BOROUGH OF BEXLEY
LIBRARIES AND MUSEUMS DEPARTMENT

London Borough of Bexley
Libraries and Museums Department
Hall Place
Bexley

© 1974 by J. A. Prichard
ISBN 0 902541 04 8

PRINTED BY G. T. WRAY LTD., ANDOVER, HANTS.

BELVEDERE

The district known as Belvedere has been called by that name only since the middle of the nineteenth century, Harris giving 1858 as the year of its adoption.* Until Victorian times there were few houses hereabouts, and certainly no village, the whole district being known by the name of its principal feature, the large tract of heathland called Lessness Heath, which stretched from Lesnes Woods and Picardy to beyond Brook Street. The district changed its name from Lessness Heath to Belvedere after Belvedere House, the principal residence, whose owners most influenced the growth of the village. In following the story of Belvedere, it is thus appropriate to consider first the history of Belvedere House and its occupants.

I

The Eardleys and Belvedere House

The original mansion was built for George Hayley in the reign of George II, to the designs of James "Athenian" Stuart, a fashionable architect of the day, who visited Rome in 1741 and Athens in 1751, and published in 1762 a volume of plates depicting the antiquities of Athens, which earned him his name. He later designed the interior of the Chapel of Greenwich Hospital. Situated to the east of Lessness Heath, Belvedere House commanded a wide view over the still rural Thames. Its name is from the Italian, meaning beautiful view. Hayley sold the house to the 6th Earl of Baltimore, who died in 1751. Upon Lord Baltimore's death Belvedere House passed to the Eardley family, who had a profound influence on the district for over a century. It was bought by Sampson Gideon, the son of Rowland Gideon, a Jew of Portuguese descent whose name was originally Abudiente. Rowland Gideon became wealthy as a West India merchant, and Sampson Gideon used his capital and influence in the City to be of service to the Government during the second

* See bibliography on p. 21.

1

Jacobite rebellion of 1745. As a reward he asked the Prime Minister, the Duke of Newcastle, for a baronetcy, but George II felt that popular prejudice would prevent him from thus honouring a Jew. Gideon, had, however, married a Christian, Jane Erwell, and their thirteen year old son, Sampson junior, had been baptised as a Christian at St. George's, Hanover Square. The King therefore allowed the title to be conferred on Sampson Gideon junior, and he received it in 1759 while still a pupil at Tonbridge School.* Sampson Gideon senior never became a Christian, although he was estranged from the Jewish community. Nevertheless at his death in 1763 it was by his own desire that he was buried "among his own people" at the Jewish burial ground at Mile End, London. His monument was later transferred to All Saints' churchyard, where it remained to become indecipherable.

When his son, Sir Sampson Gideon, Bt., succeeded to his inheritance at Belvedere House, he rebuilt the mansion so completely in 1764 that little of the original remained. He also laid out and improved the Park, which was enclosed by an oak fence, the whole estate comprising some 120 acres. In 1766 he married the daughter of Sir John Eardley Wilmot, by whom he had two sons and three daughters. Entering Parliament after the manner of gentlemen of his day, he served as a member for Cambridge, Coventry, and Wallingford. William Pitt, the Prime Minister, visited him at Belvedere House, and he was shortly afterwards raised to the peerage, becoming Baron Eardley of Spalding, Lincolnshire, in the peerage of Ireland, in 1789, earning from John Wilkes the gibe of being "Pitt's Jew". He died eventually on Christmas Day 1824, aged 79.

Both his sons having predeceased him unmarried, the Belvedere property passed to his eldest daughter, who married Lord Saye and Sele, whose seat the house became. He is remembered as a kindly but somewhat wild gentleman, who once amused his guests by using the best china to shy at. Their son died unmarried in 1846, and Lord Saye and Sele followed him the next year.

Lord Eardley's second daughter had married Sir Culling Smith, created a baronet in 1802, who died in 1812. He was succeeded by

* See Appendix I.

his second son, also Sir Culling Smith, who thus inherited Belvedere in 1847, upon which he took the name of Eardley. As Sir Culling Eardley he left his mark on the district, developing the estate outside the Park, and influencing the religious life of the neighbourhood with his staunch non-conformist views. He provided the sites for All Saints' Church and Nuxley Road Baptist Chapel, and founded a school in the village, known as the Middle Class Boys' School. By now Belvedere House contained a notable collection of pictures which had been begun by Sampson Gideon, some of which were transferred by Sir Culling in 1860 to the Smith family seat at Bedwell Park, Hertfordshire, and the remainder auctioned. The connection with Bedwell is commemorated to this day by the name of Bedwell Road at Belvedere. Sir Culling Eardley died in 1863 at Bedwell Park, leaving two daughters and a son at whose death in Paris in 1872 the title became extinct, but these did not live at Belvedere House, which was sold soon after Sir Culling's death.

The name of the Eardley family is marked in several places. In the north aisle of Erith Parish Church is the Eardley monument, commemorating Baron Eardley, and his son the Hon. S. E. Eardley, who died a few months before him on 25th May 1824. Belvedere has an Eardley Road, and one of its best known public houses is the Lord Eardley Arms. In the field of education the name survives in the Eardley scholarships, founded with money from the sale in 1874 of the school started by Sir Culling Eardley, which though recognised as efficient by the new Erith School Board in 1871, had never been very successful.

With Sir Culling Eardley's death Belvedere House entered on a new phase of its existence by becoming a home for merchant seamen. On 17th July 1857, a meeting presided over by the Lord Mayor of London was held at the Mansion House, which led to the formation of a charitable organization for seamen called the Shipwrecked Mariners' Society. In 1865 the Society gave £5,000, and lent £7,000, towards the cost of £12,148 required for the purchase of Belvedere House, together with 24 acres of the parkland. The mansion was converted to a home which was run by an independent committee as "The Belvedere Institution for worn out and disabled merchant seamen". The next year H.R.H. Prince

BELVEDERE AND BOSTALL

Alfred, Duke of Edinburgh, became its patron, and the title was changed to the Royal Alfred Merchant Seamen's Institution. It has been under royal patronage ever since. In 1950 the institution was granted a Royal Charter and again changed its name to the Royal Alfred Merchant Seamen's Society.

The Institution always had a number of out-pensioners as well as residents, who in early days numbered about 100. Though a notable building, the mansion had many shortcomings as a home for elderly and sometimes infirm men, and by the end of World War II there were in addition considerable arrears of maintenance. The Society therefore decided to replace Belvedere House by a modern structure designed for its purpose, and launched an appeal for funds whch was aided by the Joint Committee of the Order of St. John and British Red Cross, King George's Fund for Sailors, The Merchant Navy Welfare Board, shipping companies, and many others.

And so after more than two centuries as one of the chief landmarks of the district Belvedere House was demolished and a new building in modern style took its place. It was officially opened on 30th June 1959 by H.R.H. Princess Alexandra of Kent. The main block has 80 cabins for men able to look after themselves, and the Geoffrey Milling Wing has accommodation for 50 sick and infirm residents. There is a central kitchen and dining hall, and separate recreation rooms for the inmates. To be accepted for residence, seamen must be single men or widowers over 60 years of age, with 21 years or more at sea with a good record. The old seamen in their blue uniforms have now been a familiar sight in Belvedere and district for a hundred years, and the parkland provides the district with a pleasant stretch of open space.

II

The Village

To follow the story of Belvedere Village we must now retrace our steps to the end of the eighteenth century. To the west of Belvedere House and its park lay Lessness Heath, an extensive and irregularly shaped piece of common land with a pit on the northern side from which gravel was taken for parish use until 1874. Although the village had not developed, there were a number of farms and cottages around the edges of the heath, some of them ancient properties.

From Lessness Heath Heron Hill led downhill northwards to Picardy. At its upper end stood the Eardley Arms public house, a picturesque white walled inn with a tiled roof, much covered by creeper, which was replaced later in the nineteenth century by the present building. Another road ran east to St. John's church and on to Erith town.

To the south of the heath ran the Bedon stream, a small tributary of the Thames which is now converted to an underground drain for much of its length. A fifteenth century form of the name was Beton Well, and despite plausible conjectures about this meaning "praying well" its derivation is unknown, though the Old English "Bydan", a shallow valley, seems a probable origin. Bedonwell, also referred to in the fifteenth century as Bedynstrete, was a small hamlet reputed to have been a manor. It was held in the 14th century by the Burford family, which became extinct during the reign of Richard II, and was afterwards in the hands of the Draper family for many years. In the reign of Charles I the property was divided, and lost the title of a manor, being later subdivided still further.

On the south side of the stream was a further area of heathland, called Nuxley or Little Heath, which occupied the area around the present Belmont Primary School. The name Nuxley, sometimes spelt Naxley, is possibly a corruption of Knocksley, from Knox, a hill. Both names are remembered in nearby Little Heath Road, and Nuxley Road, as the former Bexley Road in Belvedere was renamed in March 1939. To the east of Little Heath was the Erith Parsonage Farm, the location of which is still marked by Parsonage Manorway. Up to the Reformation the advowson of the Parish of Erith was in the possession of Lesnes Abbey, and afterwards passed to the owners of the Parsonage Farm. Until the end of the nineteenth century the farm retained medieval remains indicative of its former ecclesiastical importance, including several hundred feet of surrounding wall and two ponds over 200 feet long for fish, supplied with water from Bedonwell Stream. The farm also had a walled garden and a bowling green. In the later years of the nineteenth century it belonged to the Vinson family, who were at one time sufficiently important to issue their own trade tokens in lieu of coinage, and owned much of the farmland to the south and west of the village until it was sold for building from 1930 onwards. The house itself survived to be used as auxiliary fire station in World War II, and afterwards fell gradually into final decay and was demolished.

To the west of Lessness Heath lay another tract of common called the West Heath, which meant that heathland stretched almost continuously as far as Bostall Heath.

It was the enclosure of all these heaths which made possible the development of Belvedere as a residential area. As early as 1235 Lords of the Manor had been empowered to enclose waste land, and landlords and been nibbling at the common lands ever since. Baron Eardley was leader of the movement to enclose the commons of Erith at the start of the nineteenth century, ostensibly because more agricultural land was required for the war effort against Napoleon. He began his campaign in 1809 by attempting to overawe the local vestry, who were then the governing body of the common lands. He wrung from them permission to enclose one and a half acres, and in compensation left 40 shillings a year to be distributed annually among about forty poor persons of the district. After lapsing for some years, this was revived as the Erith "Bread Charity", administered by two persons appointed by the town council and the Vicar of Erith. Lord Eardley also secured the support of other land owners, and they joined together in presenting a petition to Parliament on 1st January 1812, and by the 5th May their Bill received the Royal assent as "An act for enclosing lands in the Parish of Erith". William Custance of Cambridge was appointed commissioner to implement the Act's provisions, and he forbade the closing of fourteen public roads and announced the compensation to be allotted to the dispossessed commoners. A survey was made and a map prepared, and a public meeting held at the Green Man, Blackheath, on 23rd March 1815. About 200 acres of land in Erith were involved, including Lessness Heath and adjacent areas, and the remaining portions of Northumberland Heath. 38 acres of the latter went to William Wheatley, Lord of the Manor of Erith, while 32 acres of Lessness Heath passed to Baron Eardley and 11 more to Christ's Hospital, then the owners of Lesnes Abbey. Lesser parcels of land went to twenty-nine other persons. The Commissioner arranged for nine acres of Lessness Heath to be retained as common land, but this had been further whittled away by the time the local council were able to preserve it as Belvedere Recreation Ground. The Local Board of Health, formed in 1877, and later the Local Government Board, both decided they had no legal power over the common, and it was the Erith Urban District Council soon after its formation in 1894 which finally assumed responsibility for its preservation. Despite Lord Eardley's ostensible intention to convert the Heath to agriculture, much of it remained in its original state for many years after passing into the Eardley family's possession.

For the first half of the nineteenth century the district still possessed only a few scattered dwellings, but in 1849 the North Kent Railway opened to Erith, and provided an incentive to land owners to develop their property. In 1856 Sir Culling Eardley laid out his land outside the boundaries of Belvedere Park for building, and rural Lessness Heath was rapidly transformed into the semi-suburban village of Belvedere. Upper Belvedere was developed as a good class residential area, and apart from a few rows of cottages, the new houses were mainly large and substantial villas, many with extensive gardens. Belvedere Station was opened in 1859 to provide the new residents with ready access to the city. Gas for private and public lighting was extended to Belvedere in 1860, being supplied by the West Kent Gas Company from their Crayford Works, and then from their Erith Works when it was built in 1862. Water was still available only from wells, many of which gave a limited supply, the exception being a well in Brook Street which was inexhaustible, but from 1864 piped water was provided by the North Kent Water Company. Some of the new roads were taken over as public highways in 1869, and the remainder in 1878, the Erith Local Board of Health assuming responsibility for their maintenance.

The West Heath was sold for development in 1882, and the large houses formerly fronting Woolwich Road between Belvedere and Bostall were built. West Heath House, where the one-time owner General Hulse was visited by George IV, still survives in modified form in Woolwich Road. In later years the property belonged to the Seth-Smith family, but for many years until 1921 the house was occupied by Sir Tom Callender of cable fame. The house had extensive coach houses and stables, in which were kept the horses for a local hunt. Part of the stables was converted into a bungalow which still remains. Considerable open land was retained to the west of the house until 1924, when it too was sold for building development, and Westergate Road was made. The former Little, or Nuxley, Heath remained as farm land until the 1930's when it was also built over.

III

The Churches of Belvedere

With his interest in religious matters, it was natural for Sir Culling Eardley to provide a place of worship for the growing community at Belvedere. Described as a "zealous but liberal non-conformist", he had erected a chapel in Belvedere Park soon after he inherited the estate. Known as the "Tower Church", from the tower which also gave its name to Tower House, whose site is now occupied by Erith College of Technology, it was opened on 12th June 1848. It was a self-governing church, the congregation being termed "Independents", and the liturgy used was a modified version of that used in the Established Church, though the pulpit was open to preachers of all Christian denominations.

To replace the Tower Church, Sir Culling Eardley erected the church of All Saints on the heath outside the Park, and it was dedicated on 20th October 1853. He was soon in disagreement with the minister, transferred from the Tower Church, and with the Vicar of Erith, when in 1855 it was proposed to join the Church to the Church of England. After a lengthy battle conducted by pamphlets published by the various parties, this was accomplished on 10th May 1856, when the Archbishop of Canterbury licensed the Vicar of Erith to perform divine service at All Saints. Some of the congregation protested that the church was still really dissenting, and its liturgy incomplete. Lady Eardley's dying wish was for the church to be fully consecrated, and this was done on 2nd August 1861 by the Archbishop of Canterbury, Dr. John Bird. Sir Culling made a gift of the church, with its parsonage house and its schoolroom, which had cost him altogether £6,000 to build. The tower was erected in memory of his wife, and the transepts were added in 1864, since when the flint-walled church, with its substantial Victorian vicarage and churchyard trees, has changed but little. There are memorials to Sir Culling Eardley and Lady Eardley in the north aisle. All Saints became an ecclesiastical parish when Erith parish was divided into three in 1861, and comprised Upper and Lower Belvedere, together with the Abbey Wood and Bostall areas.

Early though he was Sir Culling Eardley did not provide the first place of worship in Belvedere: that distinction belongs to the Baptists. On August 10th 1800 two young Baptist evangelists, one John Chin, the other unknown, were crossing Lessness Heath on their way to a preaching engagement at Erith, when they stopped there to hold an open-air meeting. From this modest beginning the Baptist community at Belvedere originated. John Chin became pastor of a church in Southwark in 1807, but in the meanwhile the work at Lessness Heath had been continued by Benjamin Lloyd, a native of Chatham and a member of the Woolwich Baptists. A small group of Baptists was formed but they encountered opposition, and met in various local houses in turn. Eventually they used a wooden building erected for them by a local carpenter at a rent of £5 per annum, and soon afterwards purchased it for themselves. In 1805 they replaced it at a cost of £300 by the chapel which still stands in Nuxley Road, and is the second oldest church in Erith. It probably stands on the site of two previous cottages, whose sculleries remain as small rooms behind the existing building. The church was actually formed on 5th November 1805, of six persons.

The church was of the strict, that is restricted communion, Baptists, but a rift occurred in 1862, when Pastor Davis favoured the open communion Baptists, and left to found a new chapel nearby. Despite the division the original chapel continued to flourish, and a Sunday school room was added in 1921. Although superficially damaged by a flying bomb and a V2 rocket during the second World War the chapel still retains its simple but dignified appearance, and is often referred to as the old Baptist chapel.

By the middle of the nineteenth century, there was some desire for an open communion Baptist chapel in Belvedere, the supporters of the idea including the Rev. Ebenezer Davis, pastor of the strict chapel, as mentioned above. The group wished to found a separate chapel, and Mr. Davis appealed for help to Sir Culling Eardley. In his letter of reply sent on 26th September 1862 Sir Culling said: "I have made up my mind to meet the wishes of yourself and your friends, and to give you the promised site for an open communion Baptist Chapel, in the Bexley Road". He also gave £50 towards the cost. Although only nine out of the twenty-five leaders of the church favoured the offer, the nine decided to accept and went ahead and launched a successful appeal for the necessary funds. Sir Culling Eardley was unable to lay the first stone himself as had been arranged on 23rd April 1863, owing to illness, and he died a month later. The church opened for worship on 29th September 1863, but the following year Mr. Davis surprisingly withdrew as pastor. His successor had been in office less than a week when the chapel was damaged by the Gunpowder Explosion of 1st August 1864, when two powder barges on the Thames blew up and caused widespread havoc, and the services had to be transferred temporarily to the schoolroom.

Nevertheless the new church prospered, and by the turn of the century had about 250 pupils in its Sunday school, and in 1900 the chapel was enlarged and renovated, and a second schoolroom added. In his centennial history of the church, Mr. Knight evocatively portrays its activities in the still rural Belvedere of Edwardian days, with Sunday school treats held at Parsonage Farm and Bostall Woods, and the church band performing at open air services held near the old forge beside the Eardley Arms. Sterner times were soon to follow, and in 1914 the church was organizing entertainments for the soldiers encamped on Bostall Heath, and in the

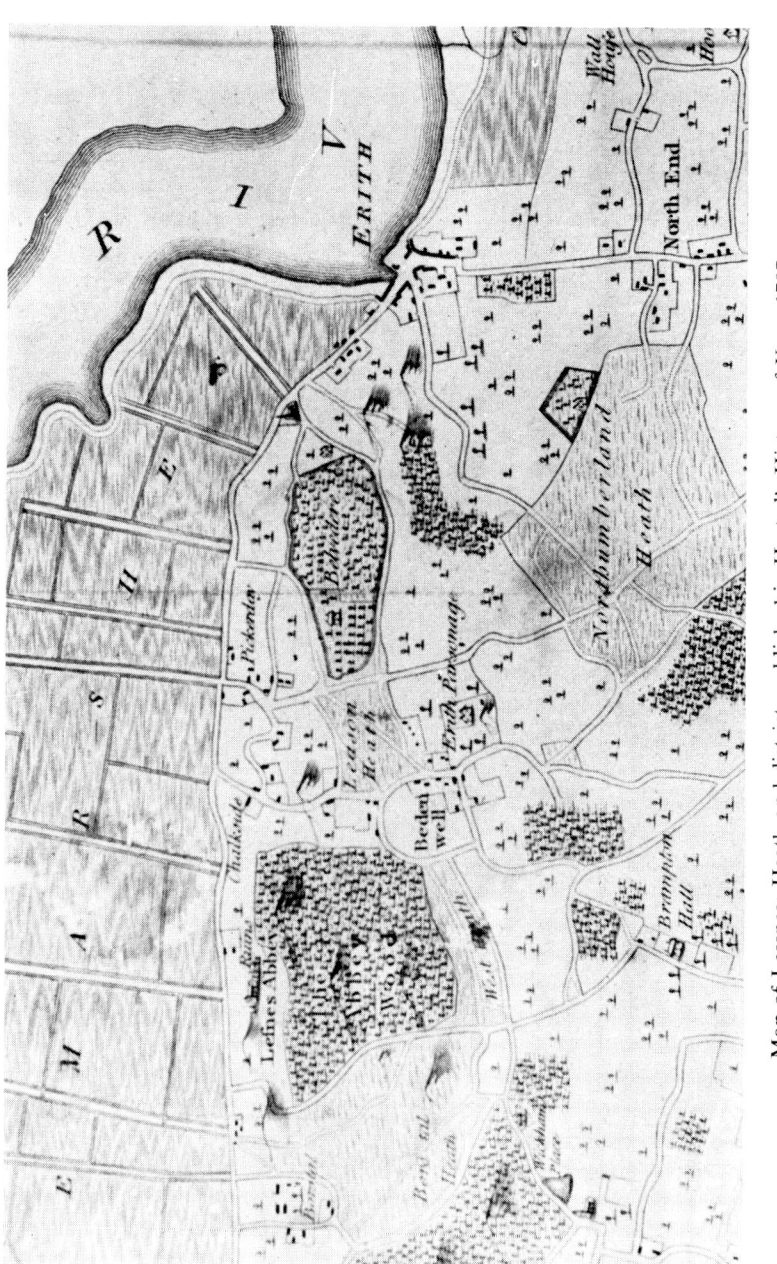

Map of Lessness Heath and district, published in Hasted's History of Kent, 1797.

Belvedere House in 1794, from an engraving by Middiman.

Bedonwell Road, near junction with Nuxley Road, about 1900.

Station Road, looking towards Belvedere Station, about 1900, when the massive iron street toilet had recently been erected.

grounds of Lessness Park nearby. The Second World War brought greater troubles, for on 20th March 1941 the church and school were wrecked by the blast of a nearby bomb, and for several years services were transferred to the Coffee Tavern and the local Co-operative Hall. After the war the new church and school were built on the site of the old, and opened in September 1950.

The other non-conformist denominations soon followed the Baptists in Belvedere, and in turn erected their typically Victorian buildings in Picardy Road. The Methodist church at the lower end was built in 1876, and belonged originally to the primitive Methodist branch of the church. The more ornate Congregational church was built in 1897, replacing an earlier iron structure dating from 1865 which stood nearby.

The social needs of Victorian Belvedere were met by two establishments still surviving. As an alternative to the public house, there was the Coffee Tavern in Nuxley Road, run by a management committee under the chairmanship of Charles Beadle for many years. For meetings and functions the Belvedere Public Hall was provided, with seating for 500 people. It was built in 1871, at a cost of £1,500, and in later years has been employed for various purposes not originally envisaged, such as a food office, clinic, school canteen, and finally as a Catholic Church, for which function its gothic style of architecture rendered it not inappropriate.

IV

Lower Belvedere

The development of Upper Belvedere as a residential district was soon followed by a similar growth of Lower Belvedere. Until the general adoption of the name Belvedere, this area was known as Picardy, a name still remaining in street names and elsewhere. The name Pyccarde Streete appears in a document of 1569, and the name is probably manorial. Conjectures as to its origin include unconvincing attempts to connect it with Puck, the sprite, and the French province of Picardy, or more probably with Pic, Old

English for a pointed hill. Picardy Road and Heron Hill led down to it from Lessness Heath, and at the foot of the latter was an old inn, the Leather Bottle, still standing today much as it was at the end of the eighteenth century, though this building replaced an earlier one which is said to have been there since the time of Henry VIII.

Heron Hill, sometimes called Herring Hill, was also the name of an ancient house standing on its slope, which was long held by the Abell family. Sir John Abell accompanied Edward I at the Siege of Caerlaverock, and his son Walter owned Footes Cray Manor. Samuel Abell was the last of the family in the reign of James I, when the property passed to the Drapers, another prominent local family. In 1725 the property was sold and divided into three. The house was in the hands of the Gilbert family from 1770 until the death of Moses Gilbert's widow in 1882, after which in 1884 it was again sold, and the land developed for building. Gilbert Road commemorates the name of the last owners of Heron Hill. Picardy Street was built on land belonging to the Parish family, a prominent family in nineteenth century Erith, which was sold by public auction at the nearby Railway Hotel in 1865.

The development of Upper Belvedere had been devoted mainly to large detached villas intended for those who kept servants and a carriage. The residents resisted the introduction of the trams and helped to preserve a secluded village atmosphere well into the twentieth century, and many of the houses were occupied by people of comparative wealth and position. In contrast Lower Belvedere was developed mainly for rows of small houses for workers in the new Thames-side factories.

To serve the growing part of All Saints' Parish at Lower Belvedere, a mission church was built near the Leather Bottle in what was then called Bottle Road. Dedicated to St. Augustine, it was popularly known as the Iron Church, and was opened by the Bishop of Dover in March 1884. By the turn of the century the population of the mission district had reached 4,000, and a larger church was required. At a meeting held on 25th February 1909 a building fund was started, but the area was far from prosperous at that time, and there was much unemployment among the local factory workers. As the curate-in-charge observed, "to collect money for building a church from people on the verge of starvation was very difficult". The plans prepared by the architect C. Hodgson Fowler were altered to reduce expense, and the building of the new church was begun in October 1914. The foundation stone laid on 26th June 1915 was dedicated by the Bishop of Rochester, but the original plan for the church could not be completed until 1965. St. Augustine's became a separate parish covering Lower Belvedere and Abbey Wood in 1916.

North of the built-up area, Erith and Belvedere Marshes extend to the Thames. The Romans were probably the first to construct river embankments, and the monks of Lesnes Abbey were responsible for keeping the walls repaired during the Middle Ages and first drained the marshes effectively. Despite the effort expended on them, the walls have not always succeeded in keeping out the Thames, and from time to time the river has broken through or over them and flooded the marshes again. A disastrous inundation strained the financial resources of the Abbey from 1230 to 1240, and a serious flood occurred in 1527, when all the land submerged was not finally reclaimed for 60 years, the flooded area being shown on contemporary maps as "The great breach". In 1928 a combination of wind and tide again caused serious flooding of the marshes. Similar circumstances brought about the disaster of the night of January 31st 1953, when much of the East Coast was inundated. The whole marsh area went under water, which extended far enough to cut the railway line at Belvedere Station and flood Picardy Street. Her Majesty Queen Elizabeth II visited the flooded area on 13th February 1953. These floods hastened the end of the extensive gipsy encampment which had been a feature of the marshes for over a century.

The marshes are now dominated by perhaps the most impressive of all local industrial structures in the massive and imposing Belvedere Power Station. The site of 53 acres was purchased by the West Kent Electric Co. in 1919, but work on the building did not begin until 1954, when the Central Electricity Generating Board began operations there. This twentieth century development was linked with the remote past by the discovery on the site of the fossil bones of prehistoric animals, dug from the marshes as the foundations were excavated. The building was completed in 1962, and the official opening was made on the 12th October of that year by the Mayor of Erith. The two reinforced concrete chimneys are a prominent landmark, each rising to a height of 420 feet and weighing 6,000 tons. The tall central building houses oil-fired boilers, four low pressure and two high pressure, while in the turbine house to the West are six turbo-alternators. Cooling water is obtained from the Thames. The total capacity of the power station is 480,000 kilowatts.

V

Later Developments

When Erith Council Tramways were opened in August 1905, the route ran from Erith via Lower Road and Picardy Street to Abbey Wood, where passengers could transfer to L.C.C. trams. Lower Belvedere was also the first to enjoy a bus service. A proposal by the London General Omnibus Company for a service to Erith via Upper Belvedere was approved by the police in July 1914, but the outbreak of the first World War the following month prevented its commencement. The first bus service actually to operate to Belvedere was L.G.O.C. route 98 along the Lower Road, which the Ministry of Munitions authorized in 1915 to bring the extra workers needed for local factories. After an unsuccessful attempt by Erith Council to operate a bus service of their own, the L.G.O.C. extended their services to Upper Belvedere on 1st May 1916. They comprised route 99 from Poplar to Erith, and route 99A which was extended to Crayford. After a break of $4\frac{1}{2}$ months, route 99 from Woolwich to Erith was permanently established on the 18th August 1919.

Despite the development of the surrounding new housing estates in the years between the wars, Belvedere retained its essentially Victorian appearance until the Second World War, when German bombs started a clearance of nineteenth century buildings. The greatest damage to Belvedere was done in the air raid of the night of the 19th/20th April 1941, when a heavy bomb blasted the shops and houses in Albert Road facing the Recreation Ground, and a parachute mine effected a massive clearance at Picardy Street. Both areas were rebuilt by the Borough Council after the war with blocks of flats. At Picardy Street there was a comprehensive redevelopment; the road was straightened and widened, the Co-operative stores, which dated from 1899, were replaced by new shops, and some blocks of flats and a branch library were erected. The whole scheme was completed in 1962.

Meanwhile the large villas of Upper Belvedere had ceased to meet the housing needs of the post-war world, and from 1960 they have been progressively demolished and replaced by modern houses. In 1963 new shops began to replace their Victorian predecessors in Nuxley Road, and Upper Belvedere branch library was opened in April 1964. With the disappearance of all the surrounding farmland the village so largely created by the Eardley family was rapidly losing its original character by 1965.

BOSTALL

The Bostall district of Erith takes its name from Bostall Heath, which actually lies outside its boundary, although the name is ancient in origin. Early forms of the name were spelt Borstalle, or Burstalle, and the derivation is from the Old English burh, meaning fortified place, or borg, meaning surety, and stealle, a site or place. After many centuries the Heath thus lived up to its ancient name again, during the Second World War, when it became an anti-aircraft gun site. Partly in Plumstead Parish and partly in East Wickham, Bostall was always reputed to be a manor, and several noble families possessed it in turn, including Charles Brandon, Duke of Suffolk, in the reign of Henry VIII. With the growth of residential development during the last century the Heath was threatened, but 155 acres were saved from enclosure and placed under the control of the Metropolitan Board of Works as an open space.

The area of Erith adjacent to the Heath remained rural in character until 1930, the only houses being a few villas in Woolwich Road and West Heath Road. The years between the wars saw a spate of new development by which the built-up area of Greater London expanded rapidly into surrounding districts, and in 1930 the building of the "new estates" in the Bostall area was begun. New houses appeared in West Heath and Brampton Roads, and the same year the first of the new roads, Abbotts Walk, was marked out. Other new roads followed in rapid succession, although the Urban District Council's planning scheme and building byelaws prevented the sudden influx of speculative builders experienced in some neighbouring areas. During the 1930's an average of 495 new houses per annum were built in Erith, rising to over 800 per annum in the last two years before the war.

Several large firms covered the entire district with new roads and houses within a decade, and the former farmland and orchards were rapidly swallowed up. Messrs. Absolom covered the erstwhile cabbage fields in the Abbotts Walk – King Harolds Way area with bungalows to create what was originally known as the St. Hilary Estate. The Gray family's extensive property fronting Woolwich

BELVEDERE AND BOSTALL

Road was built on by Messrs. Thoburn, although the splendid line of trees along its frontage was preserved, and another portion survived to become West Heath recreation ground, opened by the Minister of Health, Sir Kingsley Wood, on July 2nd 1937. The fields and orchards of Dixon's farm to the south disappeared under the extensive development of Messrs. Feakes and Richards, although many of the original orchard fruit trees still survive in the gardens of the houses. Several other firms developed smaller parcels of land, and a few odd corners, such as the council estate at the Pantiles, remained to be built on until after World War II. Another council development at Elmhurst commemorates the name of the large house previously situated there. The house, like Parsonage Farm, survived to become an auxiliary fire station during the Second World War, suffering bomb damage before its final demolition to become a site originally occupied by temporary prefabricated housing. Temporary housing for bombed out families from the war also occupied West Heath Recreation ground for several years, where a collection of adapted Nissen huts was known as Nissen Way.

The original new inhabitants of Bostall were by way of being pioneers. The new houses preceded any amenities such as shops or schools (Bedonwell School did not open until 1936), and in most cases preceded the actual roads themselves. The rows of houses spread across the open fields, the building materials being delivered by a system of narrow gauge railways, while the concrete roads were made afterwards. The original residents of Abbotts Walk spent their first winter by candle light until the electricity mains were connected.

The new community was even more sternly tested during the war years from 1939-45, when the district suffered heavy damage on numerous occasions from German bombing. The most destructive incident of the blitz in Erith occurred on the night of 16th/17th April 1941, when a single parachute mine in King Harolds Way damaged 1,072 properties.

The churches of Bostall are all modern. St. Andrew's, a daughter church of All Saints, began in a wooden building in 1935, which was replaced by the present church on the same site, dating from 1957. The Catholic church of St. Thomas More also began in a temporary building, in 1936, which continued in use as the church hall after the new church replaced it in 1951. Last upon the scene were the Methodists, whose church at the Pantiles was opened in 1955. Antedating the churches by 30 years, St. Joseph's Convent was established in Woolwich Road in 1904. Its attendant Secondary School for girls grew steadily in number of pupils, and the large modern wing was added in 1956.

After six years of service from the mobile library, Bostall was provided with a permanent library service in 1939, when Erith Borough Council purchased a bungalow in King Harolds Way for conversion to a branch library.

APPENDIX 1

A letter from Sampson Gideon to his son, then a pupil at Tonbridge School. (Reprinted from D. C. Somervell's History of Tonbridge School, by permission of Faber and Faber, Ltd.)

Dear Sampson,

The King has been pleased to order his letters patent to promote you to the dignity of a baronet; it is the lowest hereditary honour but the first step. I have hopes that by your own merit you will go higher; I shall otherwise wish his majesty had not been so generous.

I have always recommended to you the practice and title of an honest man; that only will render you honourable with the wise and good, reconcile your conduct to yourself and be acceptable to God. You are allowed to charge your coat with the arms of Ulster which are in a field argent a hand gules; let them be a constant warning before your eyes that if ever you sign a bond, paper or instrument, derogating from truth, your duty to the king, or destruction to your estate, that very moment you commit a crime as much to be detested as a hand of blood.

Behave, my dear boy, as you have hitherto done towards your master, school-fellows and everybody. Remember the old proverb, 'When pride cometh then cometh shame, but with the lowly is wisdom'. Johnson in his farce points to the vice strongly—'Pride is an adder's egg laid in the breast of every man but hatched by none but fools'.

Mama, Lord and Lady Gage and sister join in joy and love to you.

                Your affectionate father,

                        SAMPSON GIDEON.

Show this with our compliments to Mr. Cawthorne, then keep it clean till you come home.

APPENDIX 2

ARMS OF EARDLEY

The original arms of Eardley were those of the Gideon family, as follows.

> Party per chevron, vert and or: in chief, a rose or, between two fleurs-de-lis argent; in base, a lion rampant, regardant, azure.

Following the succession of the name through the female line, first to Saye and Seal, and then to Culling Smith, the arms underwent several modifications by being combined with the arms of those families, and various crests and supporters were added also. The arms of Sir Culling Eardley were

> Quarterly: 1st and 4th, argent, on a chevron, azure, three garbs, or, a canton, gules, charged with a fret of the first (for Eardley): 2nd and 3rd, vert, three acorns slipped, or (for Smith).

These later elements feature in the arms as depicted on the sign of the present Eardley Arms public house.

Explanation of heraldic terms:

Argent:	silver
Azure:	blue
Canton:	small square division at top left
Fret:	a device in appearance like a diamond and cross interlaced
Garbs:	wheatsheaves
Gules:	red
Or:	gold
Quarterly:	divided into four
Vert:	green.

The original Eardley motto was Non nobis solum (Not for ourselves alone).

APPENDIX 3

SELECT BIBLIOGRAPY

J. HARRIS:	The parish of Erith in ancient and modern times. (1885)
A. S. MCMILLAN:	The Royal Alfred story. (1965)
C. J. SMITH:	Erith; its natural, civil, and ecclesiastical history. (1873)
I. D. STRICKLAND:	One hundred years' history of All Saints' Church, Belvedere. (In parish magazine of that church, 1957-58.)
J. K. WALLENBERG:	Kentish place-names. (1931) The place-names of Kent. (1934)
J. W. WILKINSON:	Notes on the history of Erith. (In parish magazine of St. John the Baptist, Erith, 1946-1960)

INDEX

Abell family, 12.
Abbotts Walk, 16, 17.
Air raids, 10, 11, 14, 15, 16, 17.
Albert Road, 15

Baltimore, 6th Earl of, 1.
Beadle, Charles, 11.
Bedonwell, 5, 6.
— Manor, 5.
— School, 17.
Bedwell Park, 3.
— Road, 3.
Belvedere House, 1-4.
— Power Station, 13, 14.
— Public Hall, 11.
— Railway station, 7.
— Recreation Ground, 7.
Bostall, 16-18.
— Heath, 10, 16.
— Manor, 16.
Bottle Road, 12.
Bus service, 14.

Callender, Sir Tom, 8.
Chin, John, 9.
Churches and chapels,
  Anglican:
    All Saints, 3, 8, 9, 12, 17.
    St. Andrew's, 17.
    St. Augustine's, 12, 13.
  Baptist:
    Nuxley Road, 3, 9, 10.
  Congregational, 11.
  Independent (the Tower
    Church), 8.
  Methodist, 11, 18.
  Roman Catholic, 11, 18.
Coffee Tavern, 11.

Davis, Pastor Ebenezer, 9, 10.
Dixon's farm, 17.
Draper family, 5, 12.

Eardley, arms of, 20.
— , 1st Baron, 2, 6, 7, 19.
— , Sir Culling, 3, 7-10.
— monument, 3.
— Road, 3.
— scholarships, 3.
"Eardley Arms" P.H., 3, 5, 10, 20.
Elmhurst, 17.
Enclosures, 6, 7.
Erith Bread Charity, 6.
— Local Board, 7.
— Parsonage Farm, 5, 6, 10, 17.
— U.D.C., 7.

Floods, 13.
Fossils, 14.

Gas, 7.
Gideon, Rowland, 1.
— , Sampson, senior 1-3.
— , Sampson, Junior, 1st Baron
    Eardley, 2, 6, 7, 19.

Gilbert family, 12.
— Road, 12.
Gray family, 16.
Gunpowder explosion, 10.

Hayley, George, 1.
Heron Hill, 5, 12.
Hulse, General, 8.

King Harolds Way, 16, 17, 18.

"Leather Bottle" P.H., 12.
Lesnes Abbey, 13.
Lessness Heath, 1, 4, 7.
Libraries, 15, 18.
Little Heath, 5, 8.
— — Road, 5.
Lloyd, Benjamin, 9.
Local Board, Erith, 7.

Marshes, 13.

Nissen Way, 17.
North Kent Railway, 7.
Nuxley Heath, 5, 8.
— Road, 5, 15.

Pantiles estate, 17.
Parish family, 12.
Parsonage Farm, 5, 6, 10, 17.
— Manorway, 5.
Picardy, 11, 12.
— Road, 12.
— Street, 12, 14, 15.

Railway, 7.
Royal Alfred Merchant Seamen's
  Society, 4.

St. Hilary estate, 16.
St. Joseph's convent, 18.
Say and Sele, Lord, 2.
School founded by Sir C. Eardley,
  3.
Seth-Smith family, 8.
Shipwrecked Mariners' Society, 3.
Smith, Sir Culling, 2.
  (see also Eardley)
Stuart, James, 1.

Tower House, 8.
— Church, 8.
Trams, 12, 14.

Vinson family, 6.

War damage, 10, 11, 14, 15, 17.
Water supply, 7.
West Heath, 6, 8.
— House, 8.
— Recreation Ground, 17.
Westgate Road, 8.
Wilmot, Sir John Eardley, 2.
Woolwich Road, 8, 16.